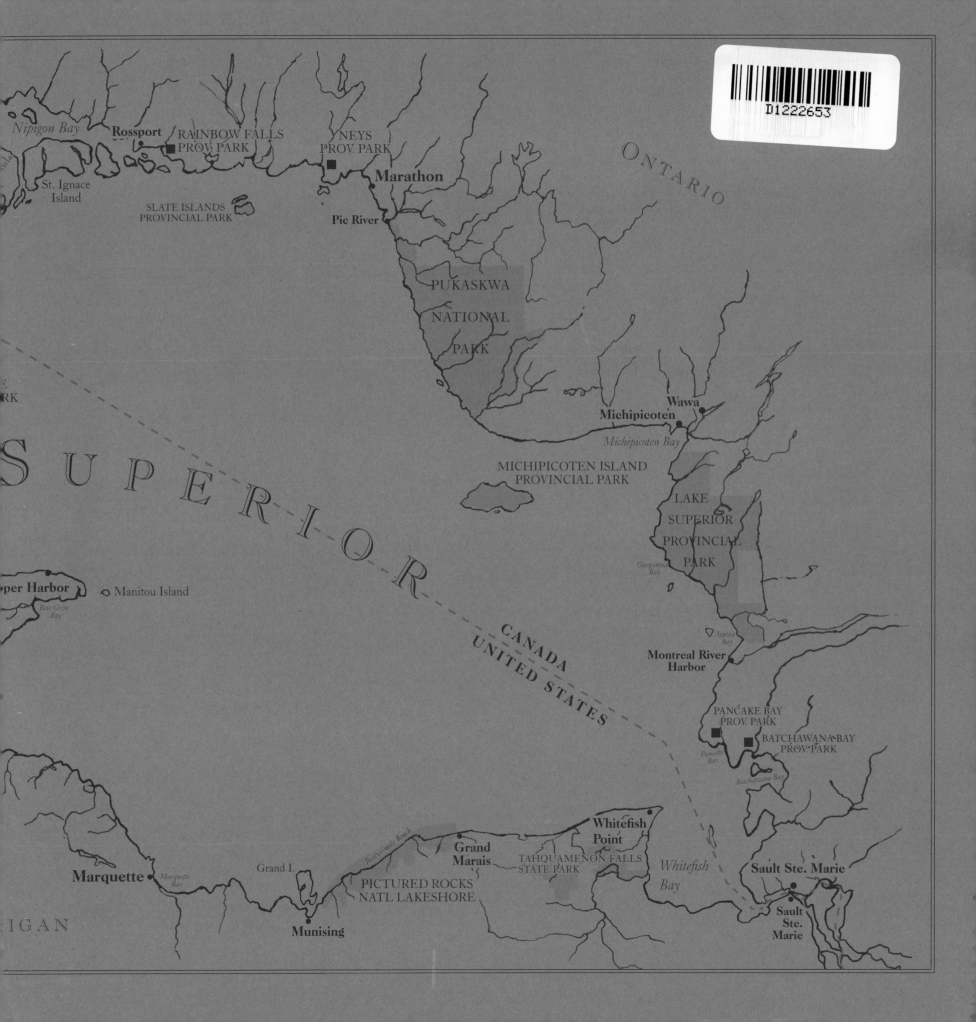

D1222653

Nipigon Bay

Rossport RAINBOW FALLS
PROV. PARK

NEYS
PROV. PARK

ONTARIO

St. Ignace
Island

Marathon

SLATE ISLANDS
PROVINCIAL PARK

Pic River

PUKASKWA

NATIONAL

PARK

S U P E R I O R

Wawa

Michipicoten

Michipicoten Bay

MICHIPICOTEN ISLAND
PROVINCIAL PARK

LAKE

SUPERIOR

PROVINCIAL

PARK

*Gargantua
Bay*

per Harbor   ○ Manitou Island

*Bête Grise
Bay*

*Agawa
Bay*

CANADA
UNITED STATES

**Montreal River
Harbor**

PANCAKE BAY
PROV. PARK

BATCHAWANA BAY
PROV. PARK

*Pancake
Bay*

Batchawana Bay

**Whitefish
Point**

**Grand
Marais**

TAHQUAMENON FALLS
STATE PARK

*Whitefish
Bay*

Sault Ste. Marie

Grand I.

Twelve-mile Beach

Marquette ●

*Marquette
Bay*

PICTURED ROCKS
NATL LAKESHORE

**Sault
Ste.
Marie**

IGAN

Munising

IN MEMORY

*For Gaylord Nelson and Martin Hanson, two men who dedicated their lives
to the health of the planet for all its citizens.*

Pure Superior

PHOTOGRAPHY BY JEFF RICHTER

ESSAYS BY SAM COOK, HOWARD PAAP, JOHN BATES AND
JUSTIN ISHERWOOD

PUBLISHED BY NATURE'S PRESS
MERCER, WISCONSIN

Pure Superior Copyright © 2009 Jeff Richter
Essays:
"A Chance of Grace" © John Bates
"Lessons Learned Along the North Shore" © Sam Cook
"By the Bright and Shining Sea" © Justin Isherwood
"Gitchigami" © Howard Paap

All rights reserved. No use or copying of any of the content
of this book is lawful without permission of the publisher.

Prints of any of these images may be ordered from the
publisher at the address below.

All images contained in this book were shot on film. No
significant computer manipulation or alteration of the
images has been used.

ISBN-13: 978-09741883-3-1; ISBN: 0-9741883-3-6

Published by Nature's Press
Jeff and Rosy Richter
PO Box 371, Mercer, WI 54547
Phone 715-476-2938
www.naturespressbooks.com

Design by Patricia Bickner, www.anewleaf-books.com
Printed in U.S.A.

First edition

CONTENTS

Methods

Yes, I'm still shooting film.

To say there's been a digital revolution in the photo industry rivals the understatements of the last century. Adding the speed and power of the computer to the capture of images has been a complete game-changer. As with most revolutions, its occurrence is easily explainable. The newfound control, instant feedback and expanded opportunities with digital capture and the photo-related software makes it very appealing to many photographers. For most uses, including commercial, portrait, and wedding photography, as well as family snapshots, digital makes perfect sense.

Unfortunately, when it comes to digital nature photography, excessively manipulated images portray a natural world that is unrecognizable to me. Real beauty, not some borderline fantasy creation made with the computer, is what makes nature so compelling.

Previous spread: Star trails in a night sky.
Above: Sandhill crane and rainbow.

My hope is that film remains viable for some time, as I'd prefer to continue shooting in a more traditional way. Each and every one of the images that appear in this book were shot on film and are an accurate representation of the conditions I encountered.

The downside to revolutions tends to be the serious unanticipated fallout that results. From my point of view, the most troubling consequences of digital capture have been the downward pressure on the value of nature photography; the contrived, artificial-looking images being marketed; and the explosion of shooters with no training and no sense of the ethics of the medium or market. As a long-time gallery director commented to me about all the new photographers coming out of the woodwork, she said, "They don't even know what they don't know." The door has been opened wide to a whole new batch of shooters whose photographic skills are perhaps marginal but they are adept with the computer.

Clearly the computer is a reality of the business and mostly for good reasons. However, to ignore the reality of the potential for abuse is simply naive. Both pros trying to maintain a level of status, as well as newcomers attempting to get noticed, have been guilty of producing images that pushed the envelope of believability.

The result, in many cases, has been an alarming cheapening of the medium in the public's perception and in the market. When it's possible to add a rainbow or an animal, or to significantly alter light and colors with the click of a button on the computer, is it any wonder the public would look with skepticism or be unimpressed by any nature photography?

I think for many photographers the computer has become an instrument for short-cutting the process and effort generally associated with producing memorable images.

I've attempted to stay above the fray to some degree by continuing to shoot film. That doesn't make me pure or completely immune to technology. I use a couple of filters (polarizer and split neutral density) that alter to some degree what the film records. Also, I know my designer has straightened a horizon or two and done some slight color adjustments that would be neither noticeable nor objectionable to most anyone.

Clearly those types of uses can and should be done with the computer. I believe when it becomes an extension of the photographer's imagination, that's when we get on shaky ground. Nothing wrong with imagination—it's the backbone of good art and good photography. But having the ability to record a subject in a unique, imaginative light or perspective is different from taking one that was shot in an unremarkable way and turning it into something it never was with the computer. That's a drastic departure from days past. Just because we *can* do something (using technology), doesn't mean we should.

When it's used to manufacture scenes that either weren't there or the photographer didn't have the skills to capture it, seems like it crosses a line. Like it or not, photography has essentially been a medium based in reality. The computer is enticing it down a road not travelled before. I worry where it leads, and for the viability of the medium in the long run.

The revolution will largely have to proceed

without me, as I continue to shoot film, using a variety of Canon 35mm film bodies and lenses ranging from 17mm to 500mm. I also shoot a medium-format camera, specifically a Pentax 645 with a 45-85 zoom lens. Occassionally, I use fill-flash for wildlife or landscape images. I've mostly been a user of Fuji slide film (ranging in speed from 50 to 400) as well as a few of Kodak's more recent Ektachromes for specific subjects.

As a nature photographer who still prefers hours spent afield working hard to capture nature's real, magical moments, I remain unimpressed, even dismayed, by a lot of the digital work I see. Digital capture and, more importantly, software such as Photoshop, have cast a long, dark shadow on nature photography that I vow to avoid as long as that's possible.

—Jeff Richter, June 2009

Pure Superior

By Jeff Richter

Where does one start when approaching a subject, a lake, as vast as Superior? Perhaps with the glaciers, sometimes over a mile thick, that gouged out the largest freshwater lake in the world. Perhaps with the billion-years-old rocks that hold its chilly waters; rocks of every size, shape and color. Granite, copper, cobble, conglomerate, slate, sandstone, greenstone and miles of sugar sand beaches. Perhaps the cold, clear waters that plunge to depths reaching over 1,300 feet. Water so pure it's still possible to drink it untreated. Water that, whenever I have the pleasure of swimming or wading in it, always refreshes my body and soul. Water so clear I've paddled a kayak on it and, at times, wondered if I was floating or flying.

Perhaps the bounty of fish that have fueled subsistence, commercial and

**Previous spread: Rocks, water and reflections.
Above: Otters feeding along edge of ice.**

sport harvesting going back hundreds of years. Perhaps the hundreds of species of birds that fly over, around, float, and nest along its shores. A feathered four-season bounty of sights and sounds.

Perhaps the rich tapestry of cultural history woven by Native Americans of many tribes, the first white Europeans, voyageurs employed by a vibrant fur trade, or sailors at the helm of ships as varied as small, wind-powered craft playing in the breezes to modern 1,000-foot freighters supplying food and steel to the world. Earlier boats moving goods by paddle and song have evolved into thousand-horsepower diesels and ipods.

Considering it takes 150-180 years for the lake to completely turn over, the blood, sweat and tears of people from the early to mid-1800s are still washing over the rapids at the Sault. Perhaps the richness of culture and ecology makes the list of subjects seemingly endless.

I'm neither geologist nor ornithologist; I'm not a historian nor any variety of academic. I'm simply an observer with camera and film attempting to tell this huge story with moments I've witnessed. I'm a collector of light, an interpreter of wildlife and landscape. I'm not a trained artist, but years spent wandering amid nature's bounty have trained my eyes to catch the moments of magic. I've developed the patience and the reflex to focus a camera lens on the edges of light, perchance to record a glimpse of the thing's soul.

It's a challenge I relish, most because it satisfies my restlessness, my love of adventure, my need to explore. My process of shooting is more instinct than intellect. My M.O. is to engage nature with an open heart and mind. At times I have specific images or locations in mind, but commonly I react

to what catches my eye, to light, texture and color that makes visual sense. Sometimes compositions scream "shoot me" while others are but a whisper that may take hours to fine tune. No matter the circumstances, the conditions of light and weather, you have to want — no, need — to get it right, to make the best image possible.

My hope, always, is to make an image that has meaning beyond what is immediately obvious. There are moments that transcend the ordinary and expected. Rare moments that are usually fleeting and difficult to capture. Images that haunt us, give us glee, make us feel connection to the natural world, change our lives. A challenge to be sure. A task a little like trying to capture the lake in your hands.

We've attempted in this collection of pictures and essays to give something of a glimpse into the immensity of both the lake and the biodiversity of the watershed. Even with the 200 or so images it really is just a snapshot, so to speak. The richness of the ecosystems could fill photography books from now until the medium no longer exists. The diversity of emotions I feel while on her shores are as far-reaching as the horizon.

It would, on the surface, seem like an idyllic way to make a living. However, for all the beauty there are equal moments of pain and frustration. Commonly, light and subjects are uncooperative, -30° temps, relentless bugs, and dangerous weather conditions are all elements that have to be dealt with or overcome. Heck — if it was easy, everybody would be doing it. People frequently say to me it must be "fun" to be a nature photographer. While I'll readily admit that I thoroughly enjoy my work, it's still work. The creative process is always a challenge and deciding what and how to market your images can definitely keep you awake at night.

While most of my time spent around the lake is solitary (simpler that way), many of my fondest memories are of times spent with my wife, Rosy, and my best buddy and photographer supreme, Steve Brimm. Rosy and I have spent countless evenings strolling various beaches around the lake watching the sun disappear in its liquid surface. Just happy to be alive and together. I'll never forget an early May walk we took at Pictured Rocks, where it was threatening snow, but we were treated to a lush carpet of greens and spring wildflowers as warming as the turquoise waters and sand beaches of the Caribbean. Because of the blustery conditions we were blessed to have both the park to ourselves and the love of each other's company. Rosy loves the lake as much as I.

Steve and I have shared many a campsite and adventures around Superior's shoreline over the last dozen or more years. His knowledge of all things wild, his innate perceptiveness about the lake and his creativity with a camera makes his company a joy. I recall a night camped out on a wild stretch of the Keweenaw. (Our camping is many times no more than a therma-rest and sleeping bag rolled out on a shore under the stars.) Sitting on a slab of rock as old as the earth itself, we were treated to a squall line of thunderstorms with almost constant lightning for an hour or two, across a black sky, that left us mesmerized. It was one of those moments so special the thought of getting a camera seemed neither necessary nor appropriate. A night spent with elemental forces that teach us humility and the value of good friends and wild places. We just sat and absorbed the power and beauty. Steve, too, loves the lake as much as I do.

Perhaps that's the goal, really — to share my feelings and what I've learned from others. To impart my love of this visual narcotic that is Lake Superior in the hope others will be so affected: others with skills in politics, organizing, scientific study, regulatory matters, or activism — visionaries who will be inspired individually and collectively to protect this national and natural treasure. There's not another one like it.

We cannot allow it to be viewed as nothing more than a highway for freighters, a super-sized bottle of drinking water, a resource to be marketed for maximum profit. Conflicts arise from people who measure wealth in material possessions and balance sheets, versus those who consider wealth of experience more valuable. The depth and breadth of value is as great as the enormity of the lake itself.

For me, the whispered fall of a moccasin, the shimmer of a rising moon, the barely audible dip and pull of a paddle or the patter of rain on a forest canopy, the dancing and blinking of northern lights, fireflies and shooting stars, the splash of a swimming child or spawning trout, winds hushed or pushing up 15-footers — these are all elements of value that don't show up on corporate financial reports. My balance sheet shows them all and hundreds more sights and experiences of thirty-plus years of recreating and almost twenty years photographing its sprawling grandeur. Perhaps the will for a sustainable lifestyle is a mindset that will take hold and allow the biodiversity of this greatest of lakes to flourish. And with it, so too, we humans. ■

Plate glass ice, Madeline Island.

Isle Royale

Gitchigami

By Howard Paap

Lake Superior is a magical and mystical place. Beauty and deep meaning can be found out on its open water and all around its shores. Today, the Pictured Rocks, Grand Sable Dunes, and pristine Isle Royale of Michigan, the Apostle Islands of Wisconsin, Minnesota's majestic North Shore, and Ontario's Sleeping Giant, Pukaskwa National Park and intriguing pictographs and petroglyphs treat us to this wonder. Historians tell us that humans have marveled at Lake Superior for hundreds of years, and archeologists say prehistoric humans lived with this lake for thousands of years. The earliest of these people left no written record, but surely they contemplated the big lake's power and magnificence. In the Apostle Island region these early humans were on the lake, and using its resources by about 8,000 B.C., and probably much earlier. Raw copper was being mined on what is now Michigan's Upper

Previous spread: Lightning strike and tree pollen on water, Apostle Islands. Above: Albino deer.

Peninsula and distant Isle Royale by at least 4-5,000 B.C., so we know human communities have been coming to the lake and its surrounding countryside for a very long time.

With few exceptions the names given this lake speak to its immense size, but for those of us contemporaries who live beside it, this is not just a big body of water. No, size is not all of what this lake is about. Lake Superior has a *primal presence* that humbles us. Whether loud or quiet, this lake speaks to all who come beside it.

In historical time the early list of tribal communities coming to this lake includes the Cree, Dakota, Ojibwe, Huron, Odawa, Iroquois, Illinois, Potawatomie, Mesquakie, Sauk, and more – and the reasons for their coming are varied, but we can be certain that when here they paused to consider their situation. Surely, they made offerings to this lake.

The first Europeans who came arrived in the early decades of the seventeenth century, and it is often said the first white man to actually visit the lake likely was Etienne Brule, who may have arrived as early as 1622. The young Frenchman, Jean Nicolet, doubtless saw its eastern expanse at Sault Ste. Marie in 1634, and the Jesuit Relations tell that seven years later two French priests, Charles Raymbault and Isaac Jogues, came to the lake's eastern outlet, making them the next in line to witness Superior.

The next Europeans to see the lake were Radisson and Groseilliers, the French fur traders who came in 1659. Medart Chouart, Sieur des Grosseilliers, and his brother-in-law, Pierre Esprit Radisson, wintered in Chequamegon Bay on that trip, and in spring they participated in an Algonquin Feast of the Dead ceremony just south of the lake that, according to Radisson's journal, involved "eighteen several nations."

Some of these early visitors, such as Radisson, Groseilliers, and the Jesuits, left written accounts of their wonder, but some, like the Ojibwe, left much more. To them, the lake became the very heart of their metaphysical being, and as stated in their oral and written teachings, *Gitchigami*, the big lake, is centrally located on their spiritual axis – their ideological and cosmological *axis mundi* – and because of this is integral to the well being of their world.

Living beside Lake Superior, daily I am reminded of these prehistoric and historic connections, and their deep meanings for some, and when venturing out onto its waters I am even more aware of this importance. There is a quiet magic reaching out to those who move amidst Lake Superior's islands and along its shores. At times of calm water this magic permeates our thoughts in welcoming ways, but in times of storms and rough seas it becomes threatening and forces us to bow before a superior form. When the big lake shows its fury, we must retreat.

Geologists say rock from the shores of Lake Superior is four and a half *billion* years old, placing it in the Pre-Cambrian Era, the first era of time on earth. This cold water has a connection with *the beginning*, and that fact contributes to its truly primal character. Lake Superior is not just big – it is also *first*.

The Ojibwe people recognize this, but they go

further. They understand *Gitchigami,* the big lake, is the abode of *Mishibizhii,* their *great* panther. This powerful spiritual figure lives in the lake and must be regularly propitiated. Superior's waters are his waters, and humans who traverse them do so at his acquiescence. In a wonderful paradox, *Nibi,* water, is essential for life, but when confronted with it to a degree as vast as that of this big lake, humans must be careful. Tobacco should be put down as a show of homage.

Lake Superior plays a major role in the Ojibwe origin belief system, for the lake holds that Madeline Island, destination of the peoples' epical westward migration from a distant saltwater sea. After an interminable time these travelers came to *Boweting,* Sault Ste. Marie, at the lake's eastern entry, and off to the west found the lake glistening before them. In time they grew comfortable with its cold and deep waters, and before long they had traversed its wide expanse, paddling all the way to its far western shore. Interestingly, today, as the lake encircles Madeline Island, in turn, the many communities of the Ojibwe people encircle the lake.

After studying Ojibwe origin teachings, Claude Levi-Strauss, the famed French anthropologist, characterized Ojibwe culture as one found within a birchbark canoe, on water, and like the sun, always moving westward. Levi-Strauss, of course, was using metaphor to suggest that the Ojibwe are a people of the water, and as such, Lake Superior is their mightiest ally. Its water is essential to their existence.

In 1826, Thomas L. McKenny, at the time the director of the Office of Indian Affairs for the still young United States, was on Lake Superior when he observed a large group of Ojibwe people coming to shore in their canoes. In his journal McKenny remarked on their expertise in handling these birchbark vessels and especially at how the woman and children were truly proficient in their ability to maneuver the thin and light craft. McKenny saw that these people were one with their big lake. They were at home on its waters – and to feel at home on Lake Superior is no little thing.

To the Ojibwe the depth of Lake Superior is juxtaposed to the height of the sky, and the polarity of these two extremes forms the vertical axis of the peoples' world. As the big lake is the abode of the powerful *Mishibishii,* the sky is the home of the powerful *Animikii,* the Thunderer. A cosmic tension runs between this bird, or thunderbird, and the underwater panther and gives a deep internal structure to Ojibwe life. When in balance, their world is a harmonious one, and at such times all forms of life are at rest. But, when times are uneasy, and when this becomes extreme, it can throw their world out of balance causing a confrontation between *Mishibishii* and *Animikii.* When these two powerful spirits are in combat with each other Lake Superior is no place for humans.

Thoughts of the living presence of these two Ojibwe spirits come to me whenever I venture out onto the big lake. If the winds are down and the waters are calm I give thanks, but if the wind is up and the waters a bit rough I am uneasy.

Above: Campfire and moonrise, Pointe Abbaye, Upper Peninsula, Michigan. Next page: Kayak in sea caves, Apostle Islands National Lakeshore.

The lake's western shores are often a deep red in color, actually picturesque, and, like some of the rocks of America's southwest, unforgettable. The Apostle Islands' "sea caves" are of this inviting bright color and receive many visitors during almost all seasons. Sentient beings, we humans are drawn to color.

And here too, just as in their stories of the cause of Lake Superior's storms, the Ojibwe provide an explanation. They say these old rocks at the lake's western expanse are colored red because of *Wenabozho*, the peoples' culture hero who loves to play tricks as he teaches them how to live. *Wenabozho*, this teacher of life, who on occasion falls prey to his own playfulness, was once scratched by the thorns of the raspberry and while writhing about in frustration and pain bled over the lakes' rocky shores giving them their distinctive color. So once again, when we go to the lake – when we see its red shores – we are reminded of primal causes. In this case it is *Wenabozho* who helps make the world as it is. And in the instance of Lake Superior's red sandstone shores, it is his foolishness that makes them beautiful.

Today Lake Superior is an integral part of ongoing life in the center of the North American continent and when caught up in our modern lives it might be easy to disregard its pre- and early historical importance, but anyone who spends a length of time on its waters or just beside its shores feels its penetrating presence. Lake Superior is a natural wonder, and like a quiet and sincere friend stands by, and when we need its solace we go to it. Its strength seems endless. ■

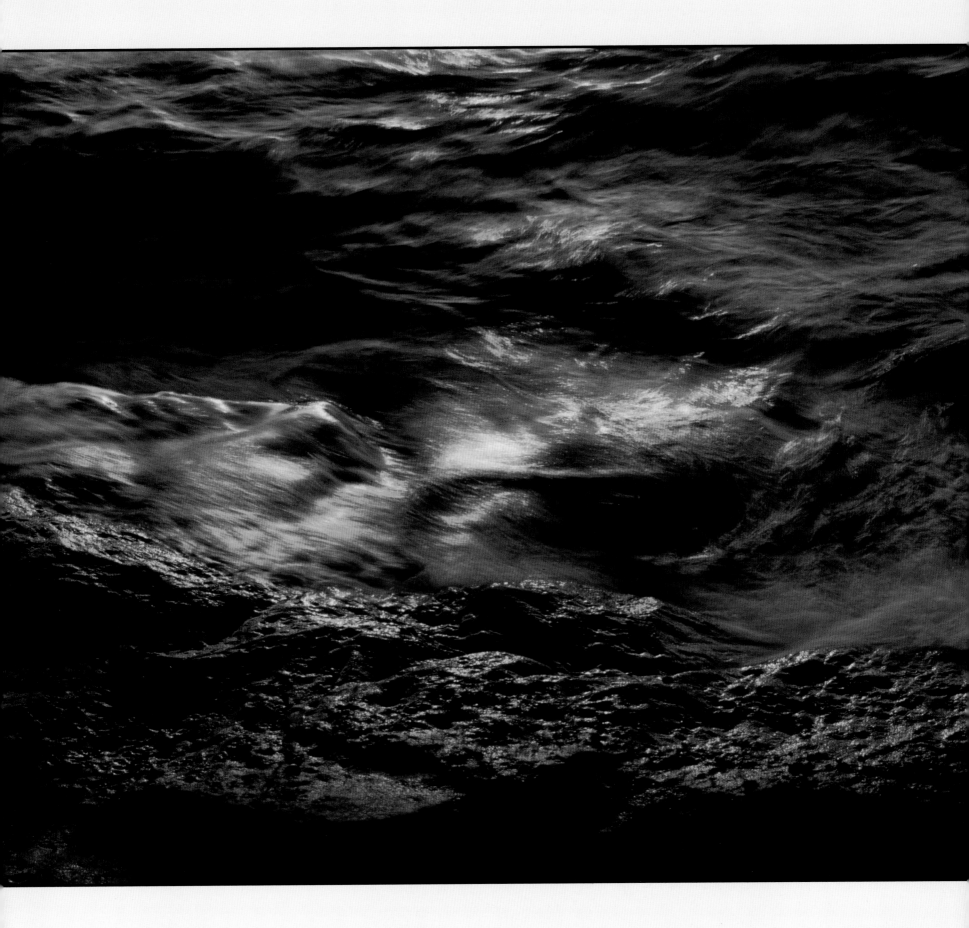

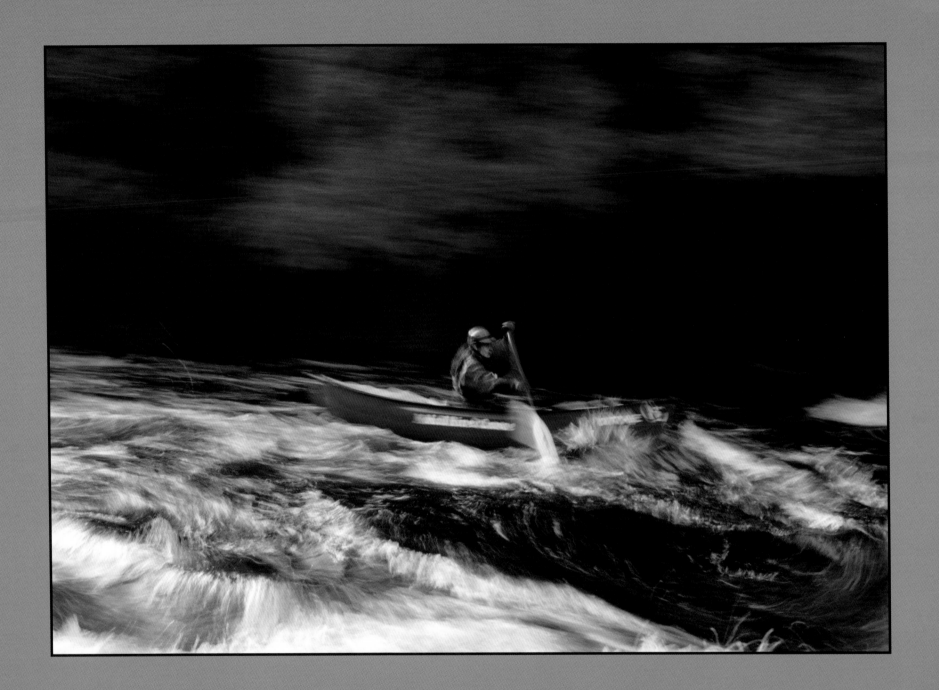

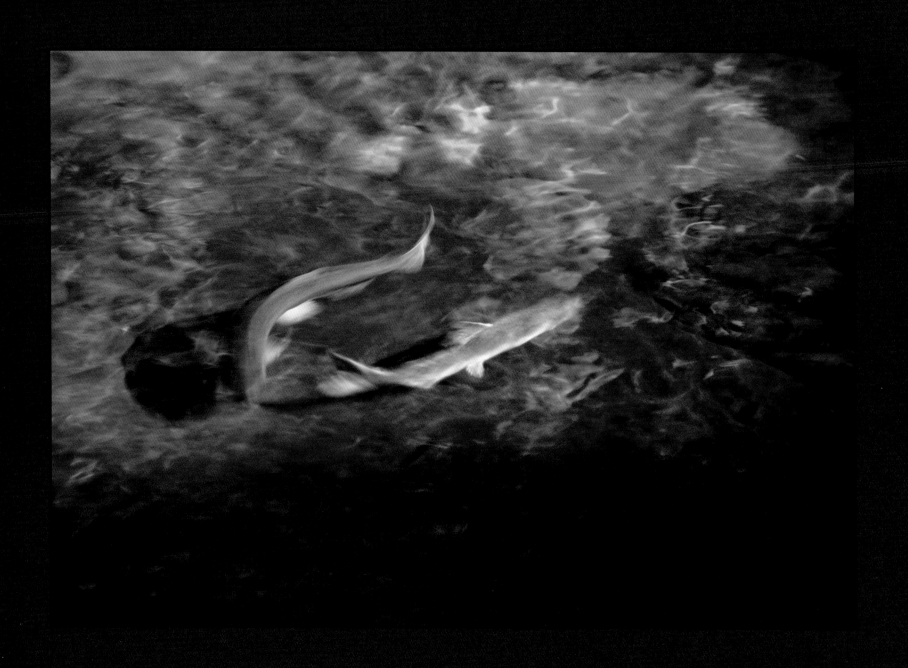

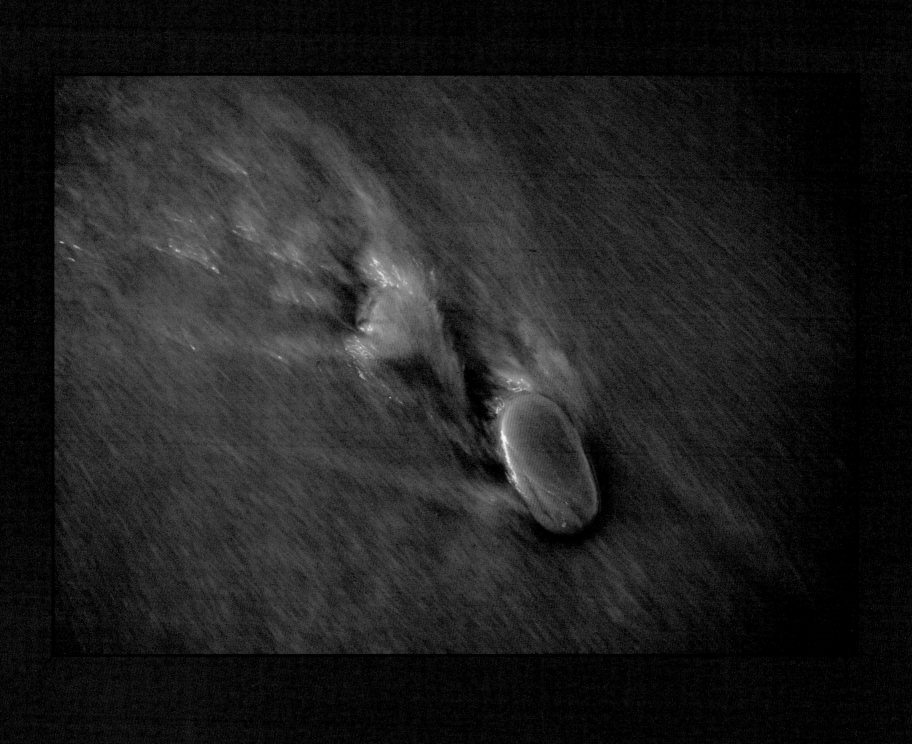

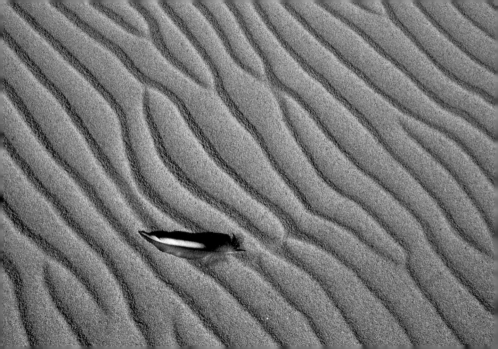

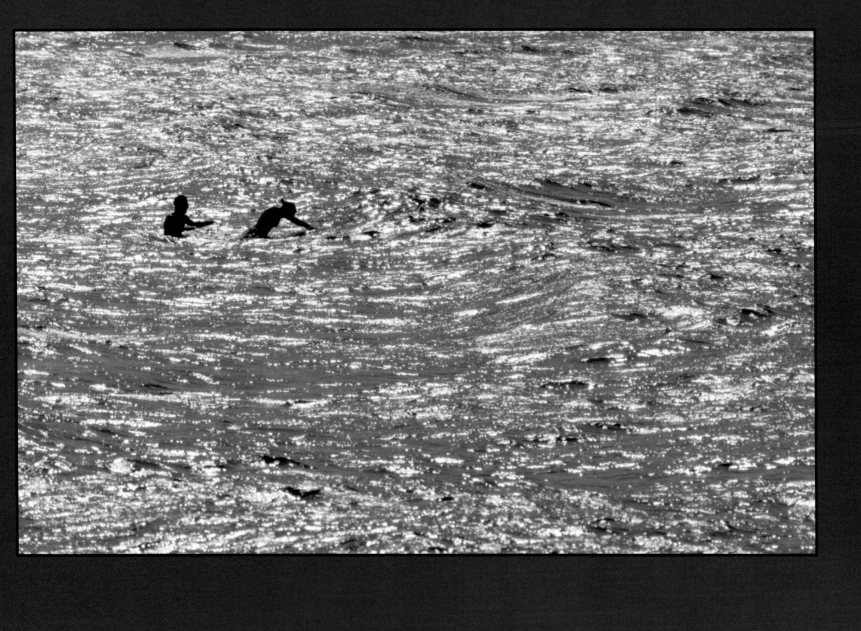

Lessons Learned along the North Shore

BY SAM COOK

Baptism

Somewhere in the dark, far below us, we could hear rollers washing ashore from the big lake, sliding onto the cobblestone beach. Three of us lay in our sleeping bags atop the cliff. We were camped near the mouth of the Baptism River on Minnesota's North Shore on an early May evening.

It had been my friend Doug's idea. We were living in Ely then, where we spent most of our free time in the Boundary Waters Canoe Area Wilderness. But Doug, a native Minnesotan, wanted to introduce me to the North Shore, and specifically to an experience known as the smelt run.

Smelt are shiny little forage fish that enter North Shore streams to spawn in

Previous spread: View from Shovel Point, Tettegouche State Park. Above: Fisherman at the mouth of Baptism River.

the spring. When they're running well, as they did in those days, it's possible to get enough for a meal or two in one swoop of a dip net.

I had grown up in Kansas, and as Doug later wrote in his account of our trip, "Cook thought smelt was something a barnyard did."

Funny guy.

We harvested our share of smelt that night, and we put them in a cooler to take back to Ely. But what remains etched in my memory now, thirty-some years later, is not the fishing but the rest of the night. While most of the smelters headed back to the highway with their overflowing coolers and pails, we climbed to a headland, threw our sleeping bags out in a small clearing and cooked fried chicken over a campstove.

Beneath us, the waves rolled in and shattered on the shore with a muffled explosion. The night was cool, and our little campfire felt good. We sat up and talked far into the night. We were young and new to the North. We wanted to learn all we could of this country. How to catch walleyes and trout. What trails to explore and lakes to paddle. What wonders we might encounter around the next bend.

This single night seemed to embody all of that, and we didn't want it to end. Finally, though, weariness overcame us and we headed for our sleeping bags. That's when we saw them.

The northern lights were out.

We lay back in our bags and stared up at the heavens for a long time, watching the wands of green light ooze and shimmer across the sky. I don't remember falling asleep, but I remember waking a couple of times during the night. The sky was still pulsing with the faint green curtains.

We learned much more that night than how to harvest smelt. We learned that when you immerse yourself in the outdoors – on the North Shore or in the Northwest Territories – you almost always come away with more than you expected. You simply put yourself out there and live in present tense. The rest will come to you.

The next time I awoke, there was dew on my sleeping bag and, in the east, the apricot light of sunrise over Lake Superior.

Humility

Big Susie Island. Summer, 1983.

We had pulled the kayaks well up onto the cobblestone beach the night before. Good thing. By morning, a northeasterly wind had stirred Lake Superior to life, and meaningful waves were slapping the stones of our little beach.

For four peaceful days, Mark and Jeff and I had sailed from Grand Marais in these modest watercraft, up the North Shore to the Pigeon River, then back to the Susie Islands. Mark and Jeff had conceived and built the kayaks, outfitting them with Fiberglass outriggers mounted on beefy supports of laminated plywood. Each was then fitted with a mast and sails.

Both boats featured open cockpits and room for two. We had motor power in case we were becalmed. Mark had a two-horsepower Johnson outboard. Jeff had an electric trolling motor.

Really, what were we thinking?

We had been warned against making this trip by at least one commercial fisherman. Don't tempt the big lake in those boats, he said. But we were young and looking for adventure.

I alternated boats each day as we sailed in light winds and fair weather up to the Pigeon River, poking in and out of bays, peering down into the crystalline water. The boats had proven seaworthy so far. With the outriggers, they were stable even in a brisk wind.

The boats were small and light enough that we could take them into the tiniest coves, and we could haul them up the beaches at night. We camped on remote crescent shorelines where few others had been. We bummed along the wave-battered shores, picking driftwood, inspecting stones. It was a good life.

We awoke that morning on Big Susie Island to a different Lake Superior. The sky was low and thick. The waves seemed to mean business. We wolfed down breakfast and decided to make the run to Hat Point, a peninsula that protects Grand Portage Bay and the village of Grand Portage, our takeout.

The waves were quartering us from the stern, and the wind was already coming up. The seas were black. Dense fog threatened to obscure Hat Point and throw us a tricky navigational challenge.

I rode with Mark that morning, and Jeff rode solo in his craft. We furled Mark's mizzen sail, and Jeff furled his jib. We didn't want to give the wind too much cloth to work with.

It was an ugly ride, especially once we lost the protection of Big Susie and began the two-and-a-half mile open-water crossing to Hat Point. The trailing waves would roll up over the stern of Mark's boat nearly to the open cockpit. Then the boat would ride down the face of the wave, and the prow of the boat would nose into the trough.

The outriggers groaned. Mark and I didn't say much. We just watched the fog roll out from the mainland and all but engulf the forested tip of Hat Point.

Jeff's boat had a 20-foot mast, and when he dropped into the trough between waves, we could see only the upper portion of his mast, a needle protruding from an angry lake.

The words of that commercial fisherman kept running through our heads. This was a big lake. People in much bigger boats than ours have felt insignificant out here.

The waves built to three and four feet. They seemed impressive from our perspective down in the kayak cockpit.

The fog never swallowed Hat Point, and finally, after an endless hour, Mark swung his tiller and we ducked into the protection of Grand Portage Bay. We were safe. We waited, watching the waves, until Jeff made the point, too. He pulled up by us.

There was no whooping or hollering. No wild celebration. No sense that we had mastered anything.

Relief was the overriding emotion.

And humility.

Had we been foolish? That's a matter of perspective, we decided. Mark and Jeff had built good boats. They had performed well in adverse conditions.

Yes, we had accepted some risk in making the trip. But what we learned that summer has been reinforced on other trips to Hudson Bay and Great Slave Lake and Alaska. The most rewarding adventures are the ones where you spend days or hours or intense minutes living outside your comfort zone.

Flowering trees frame the view from Split Rock lighthouse.

Mystery

Above: Peeking gray wolf. Right: Bull moose on the move.

Pukaskwa National Park. Ontario. The Canadian North Shore of Lake Superior. July 1992. Six of us had ridden a tugboat south along 50 miles of this wild Canadian shoreline. Now we were in three canoes decked with spray covers, paddling north along the rugged shore.

This is a wild park, where the highway runs 50 miles from the shore, and brawling rivers come tumbling out of rocky canyons down to Lake Superior. In the bays and inlets, the water has the aquamarine look of the Caribbean.

Don't be fooled. Our thermometer revealed a lake temperature of 44 degrees. Swimming was quick. Woodland caribou still roam this country, though not many. We didn't expect to see them. This shoreline, with its tiered cobble beaches, is also home of the "Pukaskwa pits." In places, the grapefruit-sized cobbles have been dug up to form hollows large enough to hold two or three people. Around some of the pits, the stones have been piled up, forming fortress-like walls.

Though various theories have been advanced, nobody knows why the pits are there. Most of the stones are dappled with slow-growing lichens, indicating that they have been in that position for a long, long time.

Paddling that shoreline, with the mysteries of the pits over one shoulder and the blue horizon of Lake Superior over the other, gives a person plenty to ponder. The sheer immensity of the lake is powerful, and if that isn't enough, you paddle along the cliffs and the coves with an almost palpable sense of those who have come before.

We built our little fires in the sand and knew that evidence of our passing would be washed away by the next storm that tossed entire bleached trees far up the beaches.

You try to travel with respect in such places, not to come with foregone conclusions but a sense of openness to the country and what it might offer.

One morning, we were paddling along the shore when we saw an animal swimming from an island to the mainland. We were too far off to make it out for sure. Bear? Moose? Deer?

Paddling hard to get closer, we watched the small, dark shape until it neared shore. It climbed out and found its footing on the cobblestones.

A single caribou.

This was a moment we had hoped for. The caribou, fully antlered, shook itself to shed the cold water. Then it did something none of us had ever seen an animal do before. It looked over its shoulder at us, then looked away, rocked back on its haunches, then vaulted ahead and trotted into the forest. There was something in its movement that nearly stole your breath.

I've since come across a passage that Barry Lopez wrote in "Arctic Dreams." He is talking about traveling in a new landscape, about being receptive to what the land might tell you. He urges a person traveling in such country "to be alert for its openings, for that moment when something sacred reveals itself within the mundane, and you know the land knows you are there."

Maybe that's what the caribou was telling us. We didn't see another one the entire trip. ■

Minnesota

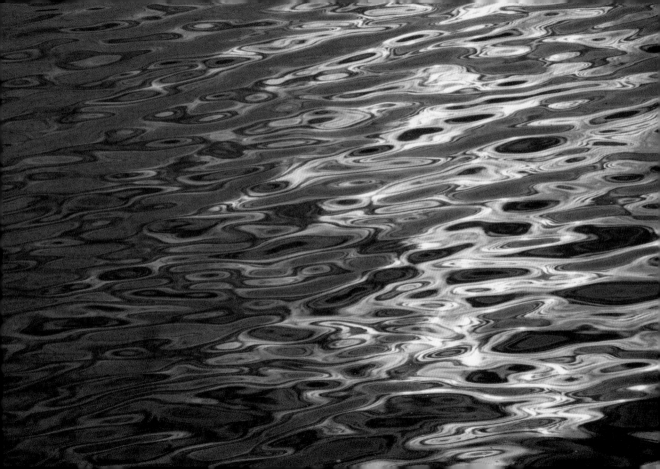

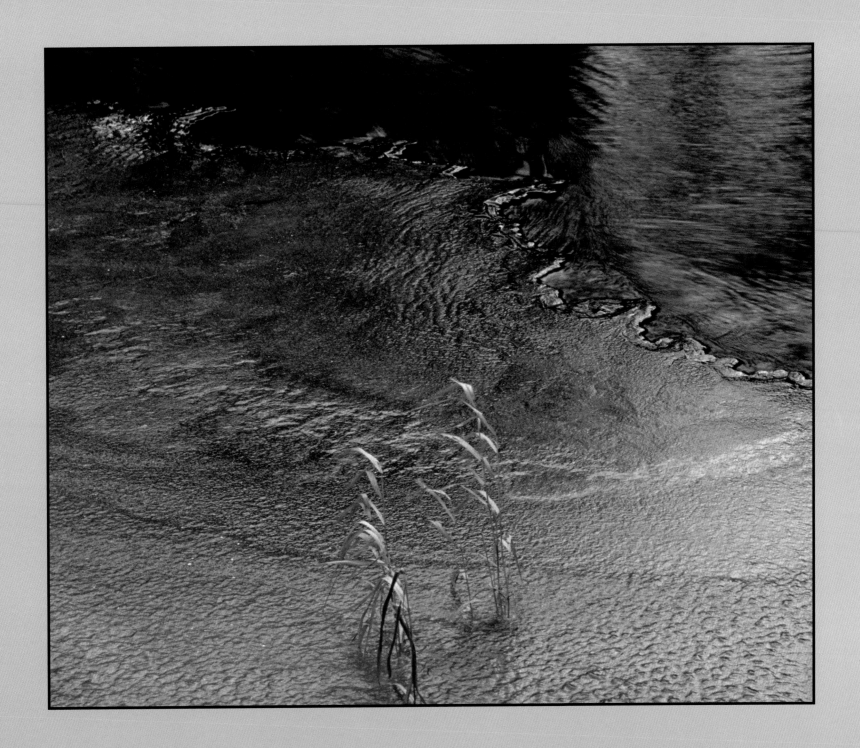

By the Bright and Shining Sea

By Justin Isherwood

Naked. A word designed to focus the attention and serve as warning, for the subject is intimate. Lake Superior is naked. Big, bold, self-defining, in-your-face, stunning, in the middle of the continent, that kind of . . . stark . . . naked.

Naked too was Superior when Etienne Brule beheld her for the first time, a Jesuit in 1618 following legends of a western sea. Father Brule who like others came ostensibly to save souls, to have a lasting impact on Superior country with its French Canadiene savore ever after, caught up in the words that sprinkle and anoint the region. We might perhaps suspect a degree of duplicity in the reverend's motives, saving souls the excuse to follow the tantalizing rumor of a western sea. The one they called Superior not because it was the biggest or the best but simply the top of the order same as baseball, she who is, Mother Superior.

Previous spread: Agawa Bay, Lake Superior Provincial Park. Above: Raccoon.

350 miles long, 160 miles wide, four hundred eighty cubic miles of water. Average temperature 40°F, 31,000 square miles surface area, 1,333 feet deep, 2,700 miles of shore line, containment enough for all the Great Lakes plus three additional Eries. Time to empty, 191 years. The largest body of fresh water on the planet. What Champlain in poetic phrase called "a sweet water sea." Equal to ten trillion 12 ounce plastic bottles, a two year supply for every man, woman and child on the planet.

What does Lake Superior mean to us in the 21st century when every resource, every lode, mode and nano-bit of Earth seems trivialized and subservient to our consumption. We who in eight hours can be half a world away, having reduced the Earth to the size of an asteroid. What the worth of a body of water equal to 10 trillion servings of brand-name bottled water whose market-researched name subconsciously connotes purity, the world's greatest single source of fresh . . . sweet water?

Lake Superior is framed by escarpments, some rising to 1,400 feet above the lake. Geologically a graben (from the German for grave), a land form differentiated by fault lines where a core sinks within the surrounding landscape creating a rift valley. Over time the rift is filled only to be exposed by glacial action. Greenstones of the Laurencian Shield have newly been found dating to 3 billion years, ranking them among the oldest features of the planet. Ironically the last of the glacial ice is thought to have melted from Superior's shore just 2,000 years ago.

When Jeff Richter called and said he was about to do a book he had threatened for some time, the one on Lake Superior, and would I contribute? I was honored to be asked— the subject is close to my heart and oddly formative of my life. For this part of the North American continent Lake Superior is a secret sharer, an emblem for the persons and institutions within her grasp. Bestowing on us a distinctive earth sense of belonging to the biggest, blue-eyed and most bodacious piece of pure water on the planet. Pardon the introduction of a Yiddish word here: *zaftig*, meaning big, bold, decidedly voluptuous, and yup . . . naked.

3,000 words is a generous allottment as words go unless you get into the subject, at which point 3,000 words is not nearly enough. The problem being the over-sized subject of Lake Superior. 3,000 words on Chequamegon Bay or the Keweenaw is no problem, but Lake Superior is like trying to condense the Universe to suitcase size. If not the entire Universe at least the center, never mind prickly cosmologists who say the Universe doesn't have a center. Maybe not, but if it did it'd be Lake Superior.

I live 150 miles south of Superior in the center of Wisconsin where my family has farmed since Black Hawk. It was the hope of this iconoclast warrior to gain the refuge of the Sault and British protection before the armed militia and U.S. Army caught up with them; Black Hawk didn't make Lake Superior. My own affair began in 1965 on a canoe trip to the Boundary Waters, the trip neatly tucked between first and second hay crop, ten delicious days away from the farm, also known as morning and evening milking. I felt well-loved by my farm father who granted me ten days in a canoe. The following year another trip to this same Superior country where I was to meet the woman I would marry. The omen now in residence, and why for one reason or season I follow Highway 13 from Wisconsin Rapids north to Ashland, a pilgrimage to fit between hay cutting or else after the potatoes are lifted and cellared. Some there are who think November is no time to visit Superior, if I have come to prefer her that way, aroused, wrathful, a hard mistress. The number of times I have been to Superior in pretty weather I can count on my brother's right hand, he the one missing fingers to a farm accident. Of places on Earth that seem to resent being held down Lake Superior is one, a personality more suited to a volcano or hurricane than polite postcard country, with a season for gales.

Once my wife and I planned to camp on the south shore where the Fox River enters, in fairness an unattractive and sandy land, jackpine, blueberries if you're lucky. A flying trip between crops, a simple box of gear, a teapot, binoculars, a volume of Emily Dickenson, we to sleep in the farm pickup. With more rain in the forecast traffic was nil, as July does it cleared enough to hatch blackflies in the warm humid air. No more had we exited the truck than we were set upon by this draculean host. The obvious solution to go swimming forgetting in our Central Wisconsin innocence a 1,333 foot deep lake doesn't warm up

like a farm pond, it might thaw but warm is another matter. In the state of pure bliss we dove in to be spit out as immediately, just short of hypothermia. Within minutes we had the gear packed in the truck, retreating to the south side of the peninsula and Michigan's bathtub water. Ordinarily antimatter doesn't get so close as to actually touch.

I have ventured this Fox River region on occasions consequent to being an English major and in turn a male animal instinctively pro- grammed to admire the reigning guy-writer, one Ernest Hemingway. And the fact he got away with literature in the same breath as boats, babes, fishing and guns. What amazed me was I could read this guy for college credit. To my mind had he stuck with Nick Adams and trout fishing and not wandered off to Spain and the Florida Keys and women in silk bathing suits, Hemingway really might have amounted to something. *The Big Two Hearted* sums up what an English major (male) needs to hear, identifies the core values; a canvas tent, a small fire, a trout rod. To whit: a thousand Winnebago campers and ten thousand condos overlooking the shore don't matter, if more to the point, shouldn't be allowed anywhere near the water. Hemingway found his Huck Finn on the Big Two Hearted, if only to hold on a little longer and it have come to him, what birders and trappers know. Still I am content. Had Hemingway expanded Nick Adams only to attract more tourists who are statistically more inclined to Winnebagos than canvas tents, Superior and her country be a different place, less jackpine, less ravens, more concrete.

Pileated woodpecker.

Boardwalk, Pukaskwa National Park.

"Nick had one good trout. He did not care about getting many trout. Now the stream was shallow and wide. There were trees along both sides."

— *Big Two Hearted River*, Ernest Hemingway

Usually it's winter when I venture to Superior, the farm at last knowing some peace, the shed doors bolted and I have Highway 13 to myself because the skiers prefer US-51, the four-lane. Part of gaining the heart of Lake Superior is to ply my way north, patiently, one village cafe, one cross-roads tavern at a time. To slow for every small town, visit the implement dealer, the gun show at the Foreign Legion, wave at the snowplows, coffee stops, the hometown paper. To my mind the by-pass mentality cheats humanity, at least it does for English majors. Breakfast in Butternut, a beer at a tavern at Iron Bridge; doesn't matter they only have Bud Lite on tap for the chance to descend into the intrigue of tavern banter and that eternal quest, Packers versus Vikings. A friend works at the Green Bay Press Gazette who provides some groty detail about a Packer caught doing "whatever" for reasons of national security is not public knowledge. With this morsel I pay my keep at a country bar between Park Falls and Glidden. Whose authenticity is determined by the number of pickled specimens on the back counter, as disappear soon as designer beers show up. The display is mindful of a museum; pickled pigs feet, pickled eggs, pickled sausage, pickled tongue, pickled ears, pickled bananas. For the life of me I don't understand why anybody pickles a banana, Freudian if you want my opinion. Down at the far end the hyperhalion of pickles, pickled testicles. Highly recommended for a first date to sort things out. In the opposite circumstance the best therapy for a friend who's gone through a divorce, to bite in half and spit on the floor. Oddly therapeutic for both sides.

The human race is divided if not evenly between what is "north" and what is "warm." Were Lake Superior located off the south end of Lake Michigan instead of the north end, she'd be crowded to the point of seething with appreciative humanity. Lots selling for a million each, summer homes of the filthy rich lining the shores with their mansions and architectural statements. When a house becomes a statement I have some doubt it is a home any more. Lake Superior happily lies north of the comfort zone, add lake-effect snow, a growing season timed between July 2 to July 5 and summer night temperatures that nobody turns the air conditioner down to much less their refriger-ator. Lake Superior is its own pickle jar, preserved by a crude wall of omnipresent chill that keeps decent humanity at a respectful distance. Only those who have made peace with ugly hats, snow shovels, and sorrel boots allowed, and not going anywhere important on any day the weather decides isn't important. On this oath and blood bond is linkage made to a sea country called Superior.

There is a rustic contentment at holing up in a cheap motel as a Manitoba Mummifier descends, the world not so small any more. In truth reinflated because nobody is going any-where, because the 21st century just got wiped out, replaced by something if not only quaint, respectful. She and I set out on such a day, drifting snow, more coming, the pickup loaded with old plowshares. The heater turned up because for some reason I convinced her to go braless. I understand the reader does not need to know this particular ingredient but the subject is after all Lake Superior and what we are after is romance. The power of a place, to lend all that come into its presence the aura of the fabulous being.

My personal recipe starts with a pickup truck, a medium grade blizzard, bucket of fried chicken, a bottle of white wine, potato chips, cheese curds, salad stuff and braless. Somewhere on Lake Superior's flank we find a motel kept open for pulp cutters and linemen, the exterior like as not painted pink—something about pink motels is cleverly aligned with human nature. Settle in the room, turn up the thermostat, throw open the curtains and then in the comfort of garlic chips and Point beer watch the weather work. The sensation is being on the first base side of creation during the eighth inning of a no-hitter, if not much action a spectacle all the same. A day to distill our humanity against a window pane and the greatly unappreciated luxury of a wretched day.

On such treks we take our holy scrolls. Grace Lee Nute, Helen Hoover, Frances Lee Jacques, Sigurd Olson, if only Sigurd had written about death and with more allusions to sex like Annais Nin he'd have stuffed Ernest Hemingway. Sigurd was way too polite to go naked but knew about saunas all the same, the objective to get naked despite the odds are against it. When I first came to the Superior country the back roads were dotted with homemade signs advertising "sauna

and lunch $1.00." For a Methodist farm boy who believed he was born with clothes on the sauna was an awakening, a ten vowel holyjesusmother-ofgodhot awakening. My panicky friend took a household thermometer into the sauna, setting it on the rocks of the stove. When the mercury burst the tube he left and did not return, not awaiting explanation the rocks were some hotter than the air temperature.

With lots of others I should bury some of my ashes at Lake Superior, such is its focus on our lives. Lake Superior is our communal having collected our hearts and bones. Under the spell of this sweet sea the span of nature and reach of man is expressed in a modest degree of equality. Whether the story is of the Copper Culture of 6,000 years ago, who by rights ought have become the Spartans of the New World, arriving at the Iron Age in sync technically with Europe and Asia, only to add gunpowder, the wheel, a steam engine; that when Chris Columba landed he been charged for water, parking and entertainment.

Of Superior's heroes one epoch marks the zenith in human terms both artistically and for sheer animal zest . . . the age of voyageurs . . . who in terms of human prowess were the ultimate laborers to ever dwell on the planet, (my Welsh miner ancestors and their ghosts will please pardon the blasphemy). Voyageurs . . . tiny men, moccasin-soled, subsisting on boiled peas and pemmican with 180 pounds of trade goods and pelt strapped to their back, setting off at the lope of a blood-trail wolf. Like as not singing, silly idiotic songs, almost android-like beings were these voyageurs, yet no mortal cup overflowed so

Tumbling stream.

Red-tailed hawk.

abundantly, so jealously, so joyously.

As said, small men with the preference to say tiny, French Canadian mostly, what the trade referred to as "engages," less mortal beings as engines, they the fiery pistons of the first American empire. Olympian in strength, god-like stamina, none loved life more or worked so hard, or died so routinely, ruptured hernia, this to shame a hundred generations after as inferior to voyageurs.

Seeking the heroic is a requisite skill notable in English majors. As a farmer I have a multitude of reasons to feel sorry for myself, my rightful share of the economy, the unending nature of my labor; it is the example of "les voyageurs" as buoy my heart. The edge I need to cut through the excessiveness of consumerism, the upmanship of capitalism, to find something anchoring and creedal of life for its own sake, without the ribbons, the chrome, the power windows. What the voyageurs did for the song of it, despite the odds, the probability of early death, these poets of the canoe paddle marked their lives and made peace with their place.

Lake Superior is not to be sensed without its catalog of boats, what began with birch bark entered to an age of sail and is now in the realm of titans; iron ore, wheat, cement, corn, German tractors. In the dirge of Lake Superior are the names on bows as didn't arrive, the *Edmund Fitzgerald* duly noted. Beyond is a long list from the *Algoma* to the *Hudson*, the *Charles S. Price* to the *H.B. Smith*, concluded by the chill notice "with all hands."

"Then shortly after 8 o'clock she dropped off so that she came around into the trough of the sea. We had been taking seas over us right along and had been using siphons and pumps. After she got into the trough of the sea, she commenced to roll and tumble and the seas washing over her, and on account of throwing her propeller wheel out of the water and losing her headway, it became impossible for us to bring her back so as to head into the sea."
— *Marine Review*, **December 1913**

Lake Superior is a story of disasters as it is of lucky strikes, of timber enough to birth a thousand towns, a silver lode of 90% fine ore when the Comstock as saved Lincoln's Union was a mere 10% pure. Out of the blood and bones of the Superior basin have come the ingredients of the modern industrial nations at her shore. Starting with fur felt and dandy hats for cavaliers, iron of railroads and sky scrapers, steel enough for hundreds of millions of cars. Such is the potency of this sweet water pool lying in the belly of two sister nations. If she looks a virgin she is instead a very practiced madam, prostituted to the needs of her people, yet when I look over her shoulder she appears nonplussed, her serene demeanor defies the passage of 400 years. If Etienne Brule were rudely roused from his grave and led by his bones to overlook Shovel Point, would he notice any difference from the first time he took sight of this sea, despite a hundred trillion dollars in cash and currency have leaked, flowed and percolated from this wonderous place? She still looks unbowed, unbested, untrafficked, that cold is the blood of Lake Superior.

1844, William Burt a government surveyor had trouble with his compass, discovering by accident the first iron mine on Lake Superior. The Mesabi Range initially tested at 64% pure iron. The first ore cars pushed by hand had a three-yard capacity. Thousand foot ore boats now sail with 80,000 tons. In the Great Storm of November 1913, five vessels were destroyed, five stranded. In the twenty years between 1878 and 1898, 6,000 vessels were wrecked on the Great Lakes.

I am refraining here from using a word for the sake of pride. Not wanting to sound wishy-washy like a writer might when they are up against something too big, too unchewable, who in desparation resort to calling it . . . *soul.* To say that Lake Superior has soul is like coming to the dead-end of a Forest Service road because it doesn't go any farther. The option is to stop there, turn around, find your way out and leave it at that . . . as soul, what Lake Superior has. It is cowardice to resort to soul when an alternative exists, to get out of your vehicle, get out of yourself, leave the road behind and make a new trail to what is beyond soul.

That Lake Superior has this something is its power to attract tens of thousands to this remarkable, as the Germans would say "gravesite." It explains why guys like Jeff Richter drags a camera through armpit deep snow and blows an otherwise cozy weekend hoping to capture some new coordinate on an entity I am trying hard not to say outloud. To admit here a distinct shortage of synonyms; if spirit comes to mind it too is shop-worn. Originally the Hebrew word soul meant breath, things that breathed had—guess what—souls. What strikes me as fair about this is it means trout have a chance at heaven.

Like many farmkids I was injured in an accident and my sister newly married gave a book to her wounded little brother. *Song of Hiawatha* by Henry Wadsworth Longfellow, premier poet of his age, proud New Englander, friend of Hawthorne and Dickens. A poet whose literary taste seem childish now, smitten as he was with folksy rhymes mixed with nostrums of blacksmiths, desperate love and gallant Indians. Longfellow wrote Hiawatha from field notes Henry Schoolcraft collected from a Chippewa woman. As the field-bound farmkid I was captured by Hiawatha and the worship theme of the canoe. Despite I was a chrism boy Hiawatha raised sincere subtle questions of what is holy, does it include corn, canoes and fields? Besides, Hiawatha had a girlfriend and a wise grandmother, he smoked a pipe, went hunting, built canoes, and was in a matter of fact way the Indian messaiah. Tending waters, clearing the path of the canoe, not to forget trout works and gravel for spawning beds. Hiawatha as read by an eight year old was an alteration to life's meaning, the map of its conduct, and what are the chores of a messaiah.

Henry Wadsworth Longfellow, 1807-1882, at 13 published his first poem, "Mr Finney and his Turnip." The London Spectator in 1868 wrote of *Hiawatha* as "sweet, limpid poetry, to live as long as the English language." Longfellow never laid eyes on Lake Superior.

Rippled sand and wave.

Above: Waterlogged trees, Batchawana Bay. Right: Pool of water in rocks, Lake Superior Provincial Park

Henry Rowe Schoolcraft, 1793-1864, explorer, Indian agent, ethnologist. In 1820 with the Cass Expedition to Lake Superior. Appointed agent to the tribes of the region, married a Chippewa woman. Produced in his lifetime a massive collection of Indian manners, customs and stories, some lavishly illustrated. The Chippewa woman's name was "the woman of the sound of stars rising in the sky," appropos of she who gave first voice to Hiawatha.

Naked. What I seek with Lake Superior is the act of intimacy. Pilgrimages have a long spiritual tradition, the routine motive is to refine the person. It is also about the place, where intimacy comes in, the act of nakedness, of being with place, with nature, with a big lake as equals. For Western cultures the worth of place, of property is never equal to the worth of persons. And where intimacy with Lake Superior is to dispute that notion. The intimacy of place has the capacity to transform the modern high-tech, digital, nano-equipped *homo sapiens sapiens* into a participant rather than a conqueror. Lake Superior undresses us, disrobes our fashionable hierarchy to something simpler, a child-like thrill of being on the stage of a great sorcerer whose provocation reveals once more our innocence. Lake Superior is big enough and pristine enough despite its industrial role to impact us the same way it did Father Brule or Henry Schoolcraft. There is a lesson in this, if we can but tend the planet as we have tended Lake Superior, to mask our use, to grant this corner and lots of other corners of the world the power of intimacy, we shall be the stewards of Hiawatha.

The Bible asks after mankind's soul and how to tend it, the *Song of Hiawatha* asks something similar but not of man alone, instead of nature, by extension the planet. Does a place have a soul and how does it get to keep it? In the 400 years since Champlain uttered "sweet water sea" we are still trying to answer that question. Our lives, our earth are at a pivotal juncture, in the end it's not about being green or sustainable but whether in the age of six billions going on nine we are capable of saving nature? The *Song of Hiawatha* as the legend of Lake Superior is an uncomfortable inquiry; of what we can have and what we can leave alone. The question not for the aboriginal to answer but a sophisticated, cell-phone giga-equipped citizen of the latest design whose grasp is infinite and whose world can be altered with ease.

In the cellar of my farmhouse I have a wood furnace and a workshop dedicated to Wisconsin's distinctive practice of winter. I build book boxes for my grandchildren, strange turtle-backed things of red oak and pine, in the back corner of each is installed a tiny dragon. The dragon duly instructed, I tell my grandchildren, to guard and protect them. At the bottom is another box, inside is their very own copy of *Song of Hiawatha* by Longfellow, Schoolcraft and that Chippewa woman. Eventually they get other books so when they go to college to have an ample supply. Emily, Henry David, Sam Clemens, Ernest ... at the bottom of them all is *Song of Hiawatha*, "by the bright and shining sea." The rest they can figure out for themselves. ■

147

A Chance of Grace

BY JOHN BATES

*Tonight the Wind Will Be Out of the North
at 40 Knots, with Waves 10 to 12 Feet*

Imagine being a juvenile Canadian songbird. It's autumn. You're a few months old and leaving your nesting area for the first time because of an urge you can't explain, an ancient calling that you're helpless to resist. Like most songbirds, you wait for sunset, the quieting of the afternoon winds, the coolness of nightfall. As darkness descends, you feel a deep stirring, churning you into a restlessness that demands flight.

If the wind is right, up you go. You feel for the least turbulent path, the smoothest sailing, a channel in the sky not too high, not too low. Clouds may be overhead or beneath you, ahead or behind, but it's the wind that matters, and the innate guidance that tells you a front is passing that will hold the

163

Previous spread: Winter sky, east shore, Canada. Above: Silhouetted sparrow. Right: Passing rain cloud over Lake Superior.

"Wind has the power to arrive unbidden, to slip through the cracks in our houses, in our lives, and hurl us to the ground. All this makes it more like the god we purport to worship (every one of us, in our myriad religions) than anything else in the human realm of consciousness."
– Jan DeBlieu

wind true for the night. You hope the stars are visible for navigation, and while other navigational instruments are at your call, the wind will have the last word.

All is well.

And then you come to Lake Superior.

What does a young songbird feel when it first arrives at the vastness of Lake Superior? I doubt elation.

The crossing distance would be unknown, though had it a map, it would see only 160 miles of water ahead at Superior's widest, an inconsequential span for a biological class tuned to making journeys of thousands of miles.

But Lake Superior is no ordinary 160 miles. Does a migrating bird stop at the shore, reconnoiter a while, think the hard thoughts of life and death? I imagine it feeling like a soldier being told to charge a hill bristling with machine guns and with no cover to hide behind. A suicide mission for some, and perhaps for many if something unexpected transpires.

A songbird may start out in a calm sky, or with the greatest of blessings, a tailwind. But if the wind changes, a different front arrives that it could not have forecast — then what? It weighs only an ounce or so, and the wind strikes it like a moving wall. The avian flight cancellation board suddenly lights up everywhere, but where to land?

Perhaps you prefer to imagine yourself as a more powerful bird — maybe a young red-tailed hawk. Most hawks migrate during the day, surfing the wind while streaming south in a series of long glides. So, you're sailing on warm columns of wind rising from the land —

thermals — when you strike the shore of Lake Superior. Unlike the moving wind-driven wall that the songbirds may hit at night, you hit a stationary wall of cold air. The warm thermals die instantly over the icy water. The magic carpet ride rolls up, and you start to drop. You could power your way across, but you're built for sailing, not for endlessly flapping. So, you follow the shore around until the land reappears again, a long detour often hundreds of miles in length, but one based on the physics of necessity when wind loses the engine of heat.

All places have a music to them that is played with particular keynotes, the harmony of which expresses their personality, their ethos. Lake Superior arguably performs one of the planet's greatest symphonies of keynotes. And though Superior's default keynote is its water — the lake's enormity and clarity — stay put a while, and one soon feels the wind that plays so wildly above the water. The wind shapes the waves, the sand dunes, the rock, the vegetation along the shore, the cascades of driftwood littered like pick-up sticks. For me, and almost certainly for the hundreds of thousands of birds that arrive at the shore in spring and fall, the wind plays Lake Superior's most dramatic keynote.

Jan DeBlieu, in her book *Wind*, says, "Wind has unrivaled power to evoke comfort or suffering, bliss or despair, to bless with fortune, to tear apart empires, to alter lives."

Indeed. The wind over Lake Superior, with a surface area as extensive as the Mojave Desert, finds unlimited freedom to build unrelenting power, to inevitably alter lives and tear apart

empires, whether human or avian. Headwinds, crosswinds, tailwinds, thermals, downbursts, downspouts, gales, nor'easters, every wind of nearly every kind can find its calling here. This immense lake and its winds embrace every imaginable personality, caressing and nurturing one moment, ripping all things asunder at another.

I suspect birds' psyches evolved foremost from their experiences with the wind. Whether a fifth an ounce like a hummingbird, or 14 pounds like a female bald eagle, birds dance to the wind's music at all times. They must know how to use it, when to avoid it, where to find it and where it will take them.

Homer described the four original winds — Boreas, the north wind; Notus, the south wind; Eurus, the east wind; and Zephyrus, the west wind. Birds know each one intimately, like a lover, because winds are gods, givers and takers. A single storm during a night migration over open water can erase thousands of birds despite evolutionary efforts through millennia to perfect the art and science of migration.

Superior storms carry away other lives as well. A single storm may wash out one plant community, but carry new seeds, rhizomes, and tubers down the shoreline to pioneer a new one. A single storm can shift sand dunes, burying plants that have taken years to get established, while exposing new ground for seeds to begin life elsewhere. A single storm can wipe Superior's surface clean of ore boats and freighters built to withstand the worst conditions that engineers can imagine.

I've listened hundreds of times to the weather radio as it forecast a gale-force storm, my mind

Left: Driftwood and grass on lake shore.
Above: Sandhill cranes and setting sun.

How we perceive these notes — the sand, wind, rock, water, the stunning power, the wildness — resides in our quality of attention and the life experience we bring to Superior's shore.

Shipwreck, Grand Island. Right: Sandstone, Pictured Rocks National Lakeshore.

entranced by the power of 50 knot winds generating 15-foot waves, my heart thankful to not have to experience it.

All life along Lake Superior knows that at any moment the wind can rise into a scream, and like Odysseus's woes in the *Odyssey* when his shipmates opened Aeolus's bag and "the winds rushed forth," their lives can be blown away. Ecologists call Lake Superior's ecosystem "dynamic," a word that shares a root with dynamite and dynasty, and all their power and consequences.

There's no safe haven. State-endangered birds like common and Caspian terns historically nested along Lake Superior, but now with limited availability of undisturbed beaches, they've shifted to artificial islands. But no tiny island finds immunity on Lake Superior.

The federally endangered piping plover nests exclusively on sparsely vegetated beaches isolated from human disturbance. But no bird that sits exposed on a Lake Superior beach ever considers itself safe.

Offshore, winds push waters out, or bring waters in. The rare no-wind day may allow near-shore water to "warm up" — an astonishingly relative term, a highest order oxymoron, that can only be fully understood by those who regularly swim in Lake Superior.

Lake levels react daily to the push of the winds, the water washing back and forth like the slight tilting of a giant bathtub. These "seiches" approximate an ocean tide, though they listen to the wind and not the moon, and offer little predictability compared to the mathematically-charted pull of a celestial body.

Mary Oliver writes of wind in her book, *Long Life*, "Who comes, the whisperer, or the howler — the trampler, or the tender fingers of spring? It is the node of change among the fair certainties — the catalyst that can shake out our hours from quietude to rampage, or back again to beatitude."

As Oliver suggests, Lake Superior's winds act as the perfect catalytic agent, transforming the physical and biological world on, in, and around the lake, while remaining above it all, indifferent.

I have often tried to catch this catalysis in action by organizing birding trips along the south shore of Lake Superior to see what the winds might bestow, hoping for a breezy beatitude from the right direction. In the autumn, Duluth, at the far western end of the lake, assumes center stage for the migration of raptors.

The record raptor count day occurred on September 15, 2003, when 102,321 raptors glided by. More amazingly, nearly all of those birds came through in a three-hour span after the winds had changed in the early afternoon.

At Whitefish Point, a peninsula at the far eastern end of the lake, raptors soar by during both spring and fall, but the Point is best known as an extraordinary site for witnessing the comings and goings of waterfowl — some 70,000 or more will pass by the point each fall. In late August, red-necked grebes, once considered very uncommon, wing by in astonishing numbers. Up to 21,000, representing 25-45% of the estimated North American population, careen around the point on their way south.

On Brockway Mountain, just above Copper

Harbor on the Keweenaw Peninsula, the spring flight of raptors over Brockway's glorious spine of rock can elicit from birders oohs and aahs for hours on end. The volcanic bedrock runs 735 feet above Lake Superior, then dips quickly back into the water, reemerging out in the lake to form Isle Royale. Riding the updrafts rising off the exposed rock, the birds flow by right overhead or sometimes even below the ridge so we can look down on the backs of sharp-shinned hawks or into the eyes of vultures.

Come December, the birds now long gone, the blasting of Superior's winter winds creates a semi-alpine habitat on the ridge that stunts and yet supports an extraordinary number of species of trees and shrubs, and an astonishing array of unusual spring wildflowers.

And all because Lake Superior offers the expanse, the world's largest freshwater playground, for the wind to hurl and whirl itself into every shape and size and frenzy and grace imaginable. Lake Superior makes its own weather.

True, some birds — waterfowl in particular — may revel in the wildness of the big lake, may be skimming the tops of waves and shouting at the tops of their lungs for all we know. But I doubt their reveling reduces their reverence. With its symphonic, omnipotent winds, Lake Superior is a god, a freshwater Poseidon, and they know it. ■

Michigan

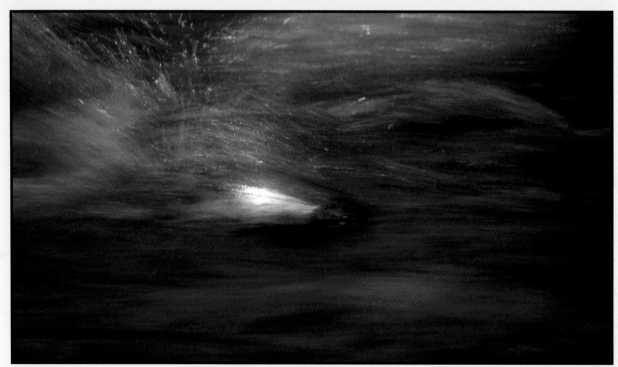

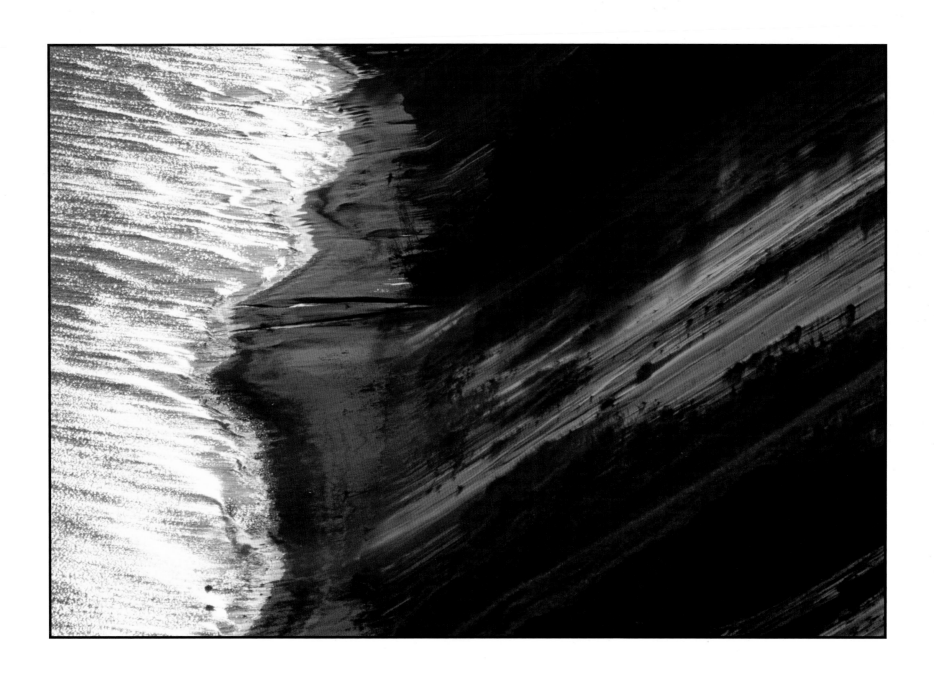

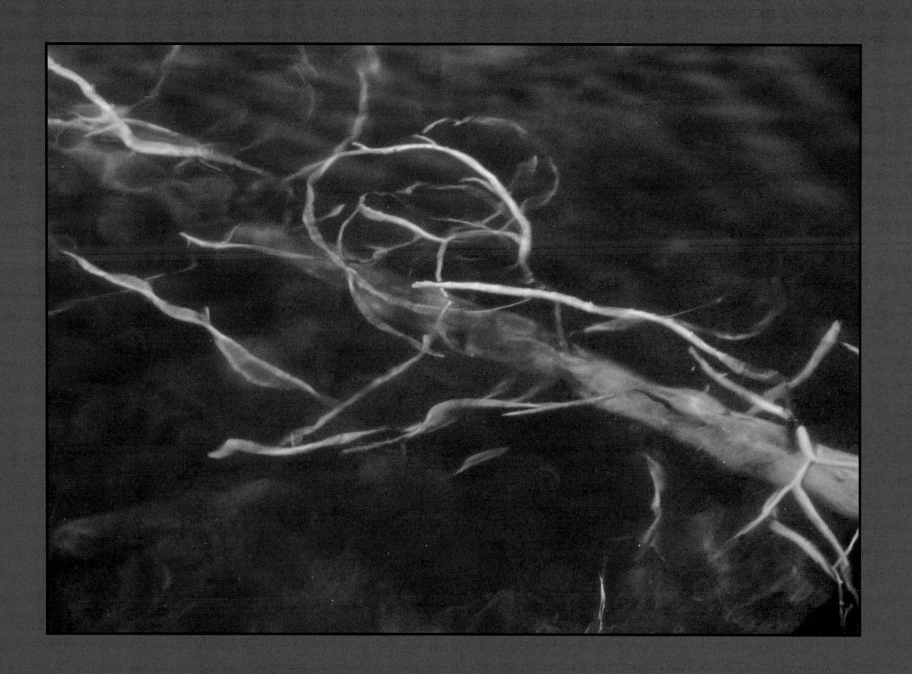

NOTES ON THE PHOTOGRAPHS

Images: Isle Royale

Page 14, Rainbow over Moskey basin
15, Black-and-white warbler
16, Ranger III entering Rock Harbor
17, Rock Harbor lighthouse
18, Caribou Island
19, Rocky cove and kayaks
20, Day hiker on trail to Lake Ritchie
21, Water lily
22, Moose antlers, Greenstone Ridge
23, Wolf in blueberry bushes
24, Rocky shoreline, Rock Harbor
26, Old growth cedar, Caribou Island
26, Middle Islands
27, Momentary break in storm clouds
28-29, Common loon taking off

Wisconsin

36, Stockton Island, Apostle Islands
37, Balancing rock, Apostle Islands
38, Fly fisherwoman in springtime
39, Mature maple trees and clouds
40, Sandhill crane in mating display;
painted turtle; backwards black bear?
41, Feeding trumpeter swan with chicks
42, Water lily
43, Fly amanita
44-45, Sandstone cliffs and Eagle Island
46, Amnicon Falls State Park
47, Ferns, forget-me-nots along stream
48, Paddler in rapids
49, Orienta Falls
50, Albino doe and fawn
51, Mature whitetail buck in fall
52, Hokenson fishhouse, Sand Bay
53, Madeline Island ferry and moon
54, Spawning trout, Sioux River, Bayfield
County
55, Beach stones and waves
56, Driftwood, Port Wing, Wisconsin
57, Multi-layered clouds, Meyers Beach
58, Ferns and moss-covered log
59, Duck feather on wind-sculpted beach
60-61, Cloudburst and rainbow,
Wisconsin Point
62, Foggy pine forest
63, Snow and ice-covered trees
64, Swimmers braving chilly waters
65, Recreational fishing
66, Gray wolf leaping over stream
67, Whitetail buck in rut

Minnesota

74, Moonrise over Split Rock lighthouse
75, Wave washing over stone beach near
Grand Marais
76, Lupine and ferns

77, Waterfall in Kadunce River canyon
78, Freighter anchored at Duluth harbor
79, Singing warbler
80, Waves, Tettegouche State Park
81, Waves, Gooseberry Falls State Park
82, Wild rose hips
83, Woods road
84, Basalt rocks, water and clouds along
breakwater, Grand Marais
85, Bush honeysuckle and cobblestone
beach, Split Rock Lighthouse State
Park
86-87, Schooner and Artist's Point,
Grand Marais
88, Rocks and shoreline, Grand Marais
89, Wave and clouds
90, Baby porcupine
91, Black bear at woods edge
92, Chasing osprey
93, Water abstract
94, Canoer near Grand Marais
95, Canada geese emerging from fog
96-97, Bald eagle on fall-colored hillside
98, Winterberry and lichen-covered trees
99, Early autumn birches near Schroeder
100, Water shimmer and clouds
101, Grass and ice forming on river's
edge
102, Dead cedar trees
103, Rock and lichen close-up
104, Winter birch, Good Harbor Bay
105, Piled-up ice in pre-dawn light

Ontario, Canada

116, Smoke-filled sky from forest fires,
Nipigon Bay
117, Ruffed grouse in autumn woods
118, Lichen-covered rocks, Neys
Provincial Park
119, Cecropia moth on lichen-covered
maple tree
120, Driftwood covered beach, Neys
Provincial Park; sunset Nipigon Bay
121, Rocky shore and approaching
storm, Lake Superior Provincial Park;
grasses and clouds
122, Sleeping Giant and reflection in
Marie Louise Lake, Sleeping Giant
Provincial Park
123, Underwater boulders and shoreline,
Rossport Island
124, Steve Brimm kayaking
125, Kingbird
126, Rising fog bank, Sleeping Giant
Provincial Park
127, Sky and shoreline in pre-dawn light,
Sleeping Giant Provincial Park

128, Great gray owl in boreal forest
129, Hiking trail, Neys Provincial Park
130, Stormy autumn sky, Peninsula Bay
131, Rossport area
132, Canada lynx
133, Cow moose with snow-covered
nose, Lake Superior Provincial Park
134, Schreiber channel
135, Backlit grasses, Rossport area
136, Grasses in ice
137, -30° day, Pukaskwa National Park
138, Old docks, Michipicoten
139, Morning fog, Rossport Island
140, Bald eagles in white pine; bobcat
141, January day, Peninsula Bay
142, Cross fox
143, Autumn storm, Marathon
144, Mouth of Sand River, Lake Superior
Provincial Park
145, End of sand beach, Pukaskwa
National Park
146, Lake Superior Provincial Park
147, Spring beauty
148, Various shots of moon
149, Shorebird silhouette
150, Large white pines, Agawa Bay
151, Cobblestone beach, Gargantua Bay
152, Tumbling water, Sand River, Lake
Superior Provincial Park
153, Agawa Bay
154, Nipigon Bay
155, Lichen-covered rocks, blueberries,
Rainbow Falls Provincial Park
156, Spirit sky, Pukaskwa National Park
157, Raven
158, Huge boulders in canyon, Sand
River
159, Old growth white pine
160, Edge of marsh, Pic River
161, Marsh close-up

Michigan

170, Blueberry bushes, Miner's Beach
173, Singing yellow-rumped warbler
172, Old metal boat, Grand Island
173, Lichen on rocks, Grand Island
174, Swooping bald eagle, spawning
rainbow trout
175, Sandstone, Pictured Rocks
176, Osprey; snapping turtle
177, Grand Sable Dunes, Pictured Rocks
178, Surfer, Marquette
179, White birch on cliff, Pictured Rocks
180-181, Same rocks in changing light,
Marquette area
182, Hurricane River, Pictured Rocks

183, Large white pine, Deerton,
Michigan
184, Female ruby-throated
hummingbird; cow and calf moose;
marsh marigolds on stream
185, Bear sow and three cubs
186, View from Sugarloaf Mountain
187, Marquette lighthouse
188, First light, Lake of the Clouds,
Porcupine Mountains State Park
189, Forest of ferns, Pictured Rocks
190, Bobcat tracks on Twelvemile Beach,
Pictured Rocks
191, Grand Sable Dunes
192-193, Various views of Pictured
Rocks
194, Breakwater, Marquette Harbor
195, 30-foot high splash
196, Bald eagle in snowstorm
197, Great gray owl
198, Wave-splashed ice on rocks, Presque
Isle Park
199, Late autumn rain, Marquette area
200, Small clearing, Pictured Rocks
201, Tahquamenon Falls
202, Indigo bunting
203, Waterfall, Presque Isle River,
Porcupine Mountains
204, Mineral-stained rock, Hunters Point
205, Beach at Bete Grise, Keweenaw
206, Fireweed
207, Dragonfly on ferns
208, Spring beauty in base of beech tree
209, View from Presque Isle Park
210, Highway 41, Keweenaw
211, Old mine building and birch trees,
Keweenaw
212, Mouth of Eagle River, Keweenaw
213, Lake and clouds at sunset
214, Evening sky, Grand Island
215, Bald eagle; mallard chicks
216, Autumn-tinged forest
217, Autumn colors on rocky shore,
Keweenaw
218, Cedar trees near Copper Harbor
219, Fresh snow on balsam fir and birch
220, Mouth of Misery River, Keweenaw
221, View from Brockway Mountain,
Keweenaw
222, Submerged tree
223, Old man's beard lichen
224, Ontonagon River
225, Ice cave near Munising, Michigan
226, -20° winter day, mouth of Presque
Isle River
227, Setting sun

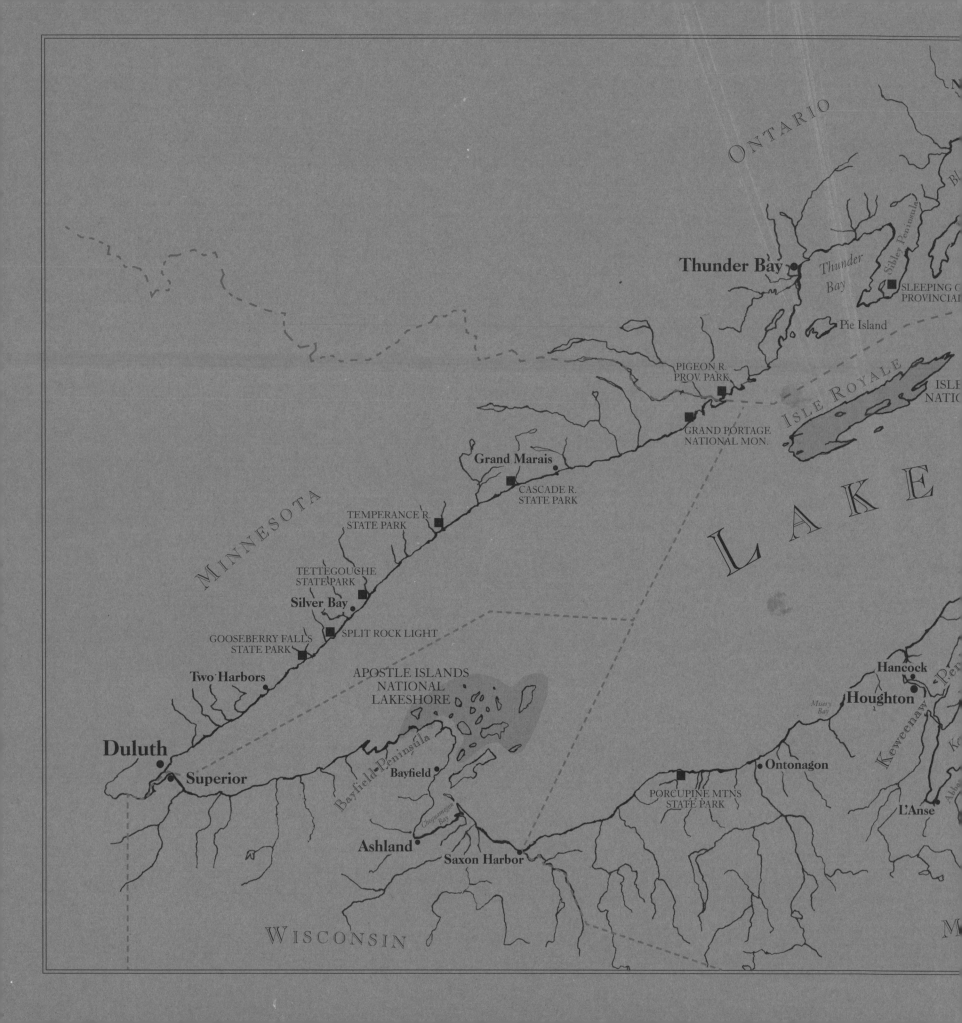

ONTARIO

Thunder Bay *Thunder Bay*

Sibley Peninsula

SLEEPING G
PROVINCIAL

Pie Island

PIGEON R.
PROV. PARK

ISLE ROYALE

ISLE
NATIO

GRAND PORTAGE
NATIONAL MON.

Grand Marais

CASCADE R.
STATE PARK

LAKE

MINNESOTA

TEMPERANCE R.
STATE PARK

TETTEGOUCHE
STATE PARK

Silver Bay

GOOSEBERRY FALLS
STATE PARK

SPLIT ROCK LIGHT

Two Harbors

APOSTLE ISLANDS
NATIONAL
LAKESHORE

Hancock

*Misery
Bay*

Houghton

Keweenaw

Duluth

Bayfield Peninsula

Bayfield

Ontonagon

Superior

*Chequamegon
Bay*

PORCUPINE MTNS
STATE PARK

L'Anse

Ashland

Saxon Harbor

WISCONSIN

M